CARDIFF TO DOWLAIS

Vic Mitchell and Keith Smith

MP Middleton Press

Front cover: A typical branch train stands at Dowlais (Cae Harris) in the early 1960s. Waiting to leave the terminus is 0-6-2T no. 5696. (Lens of Sutton coll.)

Back cover: The single line token for the route from Cwmbargoed is being surrendered to the signalman at Ystrad Mynach on 17th July 1996. Nos 37701 and 37898 are taking coal to Aberthaw Power Station. (B.Robbins)

Published March 2009

ISBN 978 1 906008 47 5

© Middleton Press, 2009

Design Deborah Esher
Typesetting Barbara Mitchell

Published by
>*Middleton Press*
>*Easebourne Lane*
>*Midhurst*
>*West Sussex*
>*GU29 9AZ*

Tel: 01730 813169
Fax: 01730 812601
Email: info@middletonpress.co.uk
www.middletonpress.co.uk

Printed in the United Kingdom by Henry Ling Limited, at the Dorset Press, Dorchester, DT1 1HD

INDEX

I. GWR map for 1947.

ACKNOWLEDGEMENTS

We are very grateful for the assistance received from many of those mentioned in the credits also to A.R.Carder, R.Caston, L.Crosier, G.Croughton, F.Hornby, J.Langford, N.Langridge, C.G.Maggs, Mr D. and Dr S.Salter, S.Vincent, T.Walsh and especially our always supportive wives, Barbara Mitchell and Janet Smith.

GEOGRAPHICAL SETTING

The docks at Cardiff developed east of the mouth of the River Taff and it was along its valley that most of the coal for export was conveyed until a tunnel was built through the east-west limestone ridge, south of Caerphilly.

The River Rhymney (pronounced Rumney) enters the Bristol Channel east of Cardiff and our route joins its valley near Caerphilly. Its main tributary passes north of the town and is known as Nant yr Aber. The Aber branch followed its course in a steep sided valley north to Senghenydd.

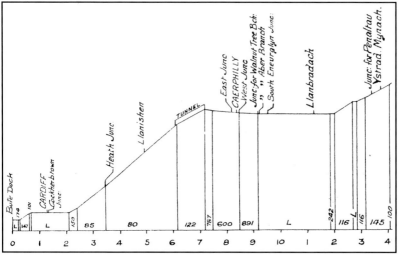

Our journey is in the Rhymney Valley from Caerphilly to Ystrad Mynach, where it climbs over high ground to enter Cwm Bargoed. This valley contains the fast flowing Bargoed Taf, a tributary of the River Taff. The final steep climb out of the valley takes us onto the almost treeless rocky uplands, which lead to the Brecon Beacons. The lines were built entirely in Glamorganshire.

The iron and coal deposits in the basin in which the valleys have been cut gave rise to the iron industry in the Dowlais/Merthyr area in the early 19th century. However, higher quality imported ores reversed the direction of the main mineral traffic flow in the next century and the old works changed to steel production.

The maps are to the scale of 25ins to 1 mile, with north at the top, unless otherwise indicated.

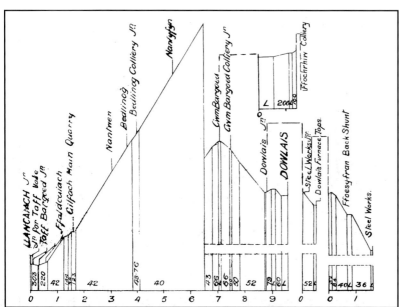

HISTORICAL BACKGROUND

The two principal lines in the area were the north-south Taff Vale Railway of 1840 and the east-west South Wales Railway of 1850. This ran from Chepstow to Swansea and became part of the Great Western Railway in 1863.

The Rhymney Railway's first Act was dated 24th July 1854 and this authorised the route north from Hengoed to Rhymney. Another in July 1855 gave powers for a link south from Hengoed to the TVR at Walnut Tree Junction, near Taffs Well, and for RR trains to run over the TVR to the docks at Cardiff.

Freight traffic started on the RR on 25th February 1858 and passenger services began on 31st March following, running between Cardiff (Adam Street) and Rhymney. Trains connected at Hengoed with the 1858 east-west branch of the Newport, Abergavenny & Hereford Railway to Quakers Yard.

An 1867 Act enabled the GWR and RR jointly to construct the Taff Bargoed line, which ran north from the NA&HR at Nelson to Dowlais. This route did not come into use until 1st February 1876, although the link with the ex-NA&HR line north of Ystrad Mynach had opened on 27th September 1871.

The year 1871 was particularly important for the RR as its own line north from Cardiff came into use on 1st April, with new connections at Caerphilly.

The single line branch from Machen to Caerphilly was opened to goods in 1864 by the Brecon & Merthyr Railway, serving various collieries and a tinplate works en route. Passenger services were operated from 1887 by the Pontypridd, Caerphilly & Newport Railway, later part of the Alexandra Docks & Railway Company, then from 1899 variously by the GWR, ADR and RR. Meantime, coal trains were worked over the PC&N, RR, B&M and GWR to Newport Docks, initially by the TVR, then from 1904 by the ADR. As the ruling gradient into Machen was 1 in 39 against the loaded coal trains, a loop line was built by the PC&N at a gradient of mostly 1 in 200, and the whole line was doubled throughout by 1891.

The Senghenydd branch was opened by the RR on 1st February 1894. The Cardiff Railway completed its line west from Heath Junction in 1909. It carried passengers from 1st March 1911 to Rhydyfelin Low Level, but the service was cut back to Coryton Halt on 20th July 1931 and the line northwards was closed. Both railways became part of the GWR in 1922 and this formed the Western Region of British Railways upon nationalisation in 1948.

Passenger service with-drawals followed thus: Caerphilly to Machen on 17th September 1956, Senghenydd branch on 2nd July 1962 and Dowlais (Cae Harris) branch on 19th June 1964. The latter line branched from the Vale of Neath route which closed one week earlier. Freight closures are given in the captions.

This left trains running from Cardiff to Coryton and to Rhymney. Following privatisation they were operated by the Cardiff Railway Co. Ltd (Prism Rail plc) from 13th October 1996. Trains had been branded "Valley Lines" since 1985. The services were run by Wales & Borders from November 2001. The operator was Arriva Trains Wales from 7th December 2003.

The Cardiff Railway had extensive trackwork at the Bute Docks and also at the 1907 Queen Alexandra Dock, seen here with one of the CR 0-6-0Ts in about 1920. It owned all these docks by that time. (GWR Magazine)

PASSENGER SERVICES

Cardiff - Rhymney

The initial timetable showed two trains daily, but an extra one on weekdays was added after three weeks. This frequency still applied in 1876, but by 1893 the figures were seven on weekdays and two on Sundays. By 1910, the frequency had risen to 14 and 4 and in 1935 it was 21 and 4. Some LNWR through coaches ran over the route until 1916.

Wartime reduction meant only 12 and 2 ran the full length in 1943, but by 1955 it was back to 25 and 8. The 1963 timetable showed 24 and 11. A regular interval service had started in the Autumn of 1953 and a 15 minute interval timetable to Bargoed started in January 2006.

Down trains run from London on most lines, but in the Welsh Valleys herein, they run downhill.

Ystrad Mynach - Dowlais

There were three trains daily at first, two of which were through from Cardiff. By 1893, there were four on weekdays (including two Cardiffs) and two on Sundays.

The 1923 timetable still showed four trains, but none on Sundays, plus some one day extras. Four or five trains were the norm for the rest of the life of the line, but an increasing proportion started at Nelson & Llancaiach.

Coryton Branch

The initial timetable had eleven weekday and five Sunday trains between Cardiff (Rhymney) and Rhydyfelin Low Level Halt. There were still ten and four in 1918, but the 1920s saw several journeys cut back to Whitchurch and Sunday trains vanished. They were all operated by steam railmotors until about 1920.

The cut-back to Coryton in 1931, brought an increase of service to 32 trips per day. The figures were 22 in 1948, 12 in 1966, 12 in 1986, but a half-hourly service has been provided since 1987.

Caerphilly - Machen

The Pontypridd, Caerphilly & Newport Railway provided the first service, this beginning on 28th December 1887 and providing three trains each way daily between the towns mentioned. It was taken over by the Alexandra Docks & Railway Company in 1897, but the line was known as the Caerphilly branch of the Brecon & Merthyr Railway. RR trains called at Machen from 1908 when three halts were opened and its service of nine railmotors began between there and Caerphilly. The GWR then ran the four trains between Newport and Pontypridd.

There were severe reductions during World War I, but recovery brought five trains run by the AD&R betwen Machen and Caerphilly or beyond by 1922. Eleven arrivals at the latter were offered by the GWR in the following year. The figure was seven in 1948, five of these calling at the halts. Their last complete year was 1955, when eight called and there was one non-stop.

January 1818

CARDIFF, LLANCAIACH, DOWLAIS, and MERTHYR.—Great Western & Rhymney Joint. [Sndys]

[Timetable — Cardiff/Llancaiach/Dowlais/Merthyr, Great Western & Rhymney Joint]

October 1912

NELSON AND LLANCAIACH and DOWLAIS.—Great Western and Rhymney Joint.

[Timetable — Nelson and Llancaiach and Dowlais, Week Days only, Up and Down]

MACHEN and CAERPHILLY (Motor Cars—One class only).—Rhymney.

[Timetable — Machen and Caerphilly, Week Days only, Down]

☞ For other Trains

	BETWEEN	PAGE
	Machen and Caerphilly	71

¶ "Halts" at Waterloo and Gwernydomen between Machen and Caerphilly.

CAERPHILLY and SENGHENYDD (Motor Cars—One class only).—Rhymney.

Up. — Week Days only.

Miles		mrn	mrn	mrn	aft	aft	aft	aft	aft	aft	aft	aft	aft
	Caerphilly ¶ ....dep.	5 5	9 7	1015	1140	1240	1 35	1 45	2 35	3 30	5 27	9 25	10 5	1120
1½	Penyrheol ¶	5 11	9 13	1021	1146	1246	1 42	1 52	2 41	3 36	5 33	9 31	1011	1124
3	Abertridwr	5 19	9 19	1027	1152	1252	1 48	1 58	2 47	3 42	5 39	9 37	1017	1129
4	Senghenydd ....arr.	5 23	9 23	1031	1156	1256	1 52	2 2	2 51	3 46	5 43	9 41	1021	1133

Down. — Week Days only.

Mls		mrn	mrn	mrn	aft	aft	aft	aft	aft	aft	aft	aft
	Senghenydd ....dep.	5 45	7 559	38	11	1215	1 25	2 30	2 55	4 55	5 53	9 55
1	Abertridwr	5 50	7 599	44	11	6 1219	1 29	2 34	2 59	4 49	5 59	8 9 59
2½	Penyrheol ¶	5 56	8 58	11	1225	1 35	2 40	3 5	4 55	5 8	15 10 3
4	Caerphilly 71 ....arr.	6 1	8 119	57	1118	1231	1 41	2 46	3 9	5 16	12 8 20	10 6

¶ "Halt" at Beddau, between Caerphilly and Penyrheol.

October 1912

CARDIFF and RHYDYFELIN (Motor Cars).—Cardiff.

Offices—Cardiff. Gen. Man., E. A. Prosser. Traffic Supt., W. J. Holloway.

Up. — Week Days. — Sundays.

Miles			
	Cardiff (Rhymney) ¶ dep.		
4½	Whitchurch ¶		
5½	Tongwynlais		
7½	Glanyllyn ¶		
9½	Upper Boat		
10½	Rhydyfelin Halt ....arr.		

Down. — Week Days. — Sundays.

Miles			
	Rhydyfelin Halt ....dep.		
1	Upper Boat ¶		
3½	Glanyllyn ¶		
5	Tongwynlais ¶		
6½	Whitchurch ¶		
10½	Cardiff (Rhymney) ..arr.		

¶ "Halts" at Heath and Rhiwbina, between Cardiff and Whitchurch; Coryton, between Whitchurch and Tongwynlais; and Nantgarw, between Glanyllyn and Upper Boat.

July 1918

CARDIFF and RHYDYFELIN—(Motor Cars—One class only).

Up. — Week Days only.

Miles			
	Cardiff (Parade) ....dep.		
4½	Whitchurch (Glam.) ¶		
5½	Tongwynlais		
7½	Glanyllyn ¶		
9½	Upper Boat ....(L.L.)		
10½	Rhydyfelin Halt ....arr.		

Down. — Week Days only.

Miles			
	Low Level.		
	Rhydyfelin Halt ....dep.		
1	Upper Boat ¶		
3	Glanyllyn ¶		
4½	Tongwynlais ¶		
6½	Whitchurch (Glam.) ¶		
10½	Cardiff A 82, 85a ..arr.		

A Parade: about 1 mile to General Station. S Saturdays only.
¶ "Halts" at Heath, (Low Level) and at Rhiwbina, between Cardiff and Whitchurch (Glam.); at Coryton (Glam.) between Whitchurch (Glam.) and Tongwynlais; and at Nantgarw (Low Level), between Glanyllyn and Upper Boat

July 1927

NELSON AND LLANCAIACH and DOWLAIS.—Great Western (late G.W. and Rhymney).

Up. — Week Days only.

Miles			
	Nelson and Llancaiach dep.		
1	Trelewis Platform		
3½	Bedling		
7	Cwm Bargoed		
9½	Dowlais (Cae Harris) ** arr.		

Down. — Week Days only.

Miles			
	Dowlais (Cae Harris) ..dep.		
2½	Cwm Bargoed		
6	Bedling		
8½	Trelewis Platform		
9½	Nelson & Llancaiach 82, arr.		

NOTES.

a Runs to Ystrad Mynach, see page 84.
E Except Saturdays.
S Saturdays only.
T Thursdays only.
** About ½ mile to Dowlais Top and over ½ mile to Dowlais Stations.

October 1923

CARDIFF and CORYTON (Rail Motor Cars—One class only)

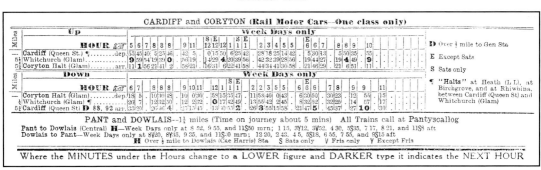

Up — Week Days only

Miles	HOUR																							
—	Cardiff (Queen St.) ¶ ....dep.																							
5½	Whitchurch (Glam.)																							
5¾	Coryton Halt (Glam.) ....arr.																							

Down — Week Days only

Miles	HOUR																						
—	Coryton Halt (Glam.) ....dep.																						
	Whitchurch (Glam.)																						
5½	Cardiff (Queen St) D 88, 92 arr.																						

D Over ½ mile to Gen Sta
E Except Sats
S Sats only
¶ "Halts" at Heath (L L), at Birchgrove, and at Rhiwbina, between Cardiff (Queen St) and Whitchurch (Glam)

PANT and DOWLAIS—1¼ miles (Time on journey about 5 mins) All Trains call at Pantyscallog
Pant to Dowlais (Central)—Week Days only at 8 52, 9 45, and 11§50 mrn; 1 15, 3¶12, 4 36, 5¶55, 7 17, 8 21, and 11§§ aft
Dowlais to Pant—Week Days only at 8¶20, 8§35, 9 35, and 11§-0 mrn; 12 20, 2 43, 4 5, 5§18, 6 55, 7 55, and 9§15 aft
H Over ½ mile to Dowlais (Cae Harris) Sta S Sats only V Fris only Y Except Fris

Where the MINUTES under the Hours change to a LOWER figure and DARKER type it indicates the NEXT HOUR

July 1933

CARDIFF BAY

II.   Scaled at 4ins to 1 mile, this map was issued by T.Waring in May 1869 and includes the RR (top centre) although this section did not open until April 1871. Lower right is its terminus, which is also shown on many later maps although it was never a passenger station. However, dock workers were conveyed on the branch. Ironically, the TVR terminus is not annotated, but is so on the next map.

➔   III.   On the left of this 1938 extract at 6ins to 1 mile is part of the Glamorganshire Canal, which was completed in 1798. Bute West Dock opened in 1839 and the TVR terminus (marked Sta.) followed in 1840. Bute East Dock was completed in 1859 and the northern section of it is the only part of the two to retain water. The canal has long gone, but the 1874 Roath Basin and 1887 Roath Dock (lower right) still exist, as do some of the tracks in the corner and also east of East Dock. At the north end of Bute East Dock is the ex-LNWR Tyndall Street goods yard and engine shed. The latter closed on 1st July 1933. The former RR engine shed is between Roath Dock and Bute East Dock, marked Terminus. It had been rebuilt by the GWR.

1.   Part of the RR engine shed is seen on 1st May 1927 along with nos 708, 211 and 161. Nearest is no. 708, ex-Barry Railway no. 37, built by Hosgood. It lasted in colliery use until 1947. (H.C.Casserley)

2.   A southward panorama over Bute East Dock in the 1930s includes some of the hydraulic equipment, which were operated by water at 850psi. There had been ten pumping stations, but only four after 1925. The lock gates were similarly powered. (ABP)

3.	The RR engine shed was rebuilt by the GWR in 1931 to the form seen here in 1951. It first closed in March 1958, but reopened in September 1962. Closure to steam came in August 1965, when coded 88M. No. 93 was an ex-RR S class 0-6-0T, numbered 608 by the GWR, but was originally 111. It was built by Hudswell Clarke in 1908. (R.M.Casserley)

This area is featured in the Middleton Press album
Cardiff Trolleybuses **and the railways are in** *Branch Lines around Barry,*
Cardiff to Swansea **and** *Gloucester to Cardiff.*

4.	The station was called Cardiff Docks until 1st July 1924 and for the next seventy years it was Bute Road. Trains from the RR 1871 route began using this former TVR route in 1928. A simple island platform was provided from about 1844 until 1929, when these two platforms came into use. No. 5641 is at the bay platform (right) on 12th September 1951, while no. 5683 waits on one of five through lines. West Dock closed in 1964 and East Dock followed in 1970. (H.C.Casserley)

5.   Turning round, we see the 1927 61-lever signal box, shortly before its closure on 26th June 1966. Only the platform on the right remained in use after that time, but the single line was moved to the other face on 19th July 1987. The Glamorgan Railway Society had use of a short disconnected length of track on the right of the platform from July 1994 until December 1996; a move to Barry Island followed. (Lens of Sutton coll.)

6.   The listed TVR headquarters building of 1843 is also in the background of picture 4. The name was changed to Cardiff Bay on 21st September 1994 and a heritage diesel railcar was provided for the shuttle service to Queen Street from 2006. Seen on 27th August 2008 is no. 121232 of 1960, which had received all the latest safety devices. (P.Jones)

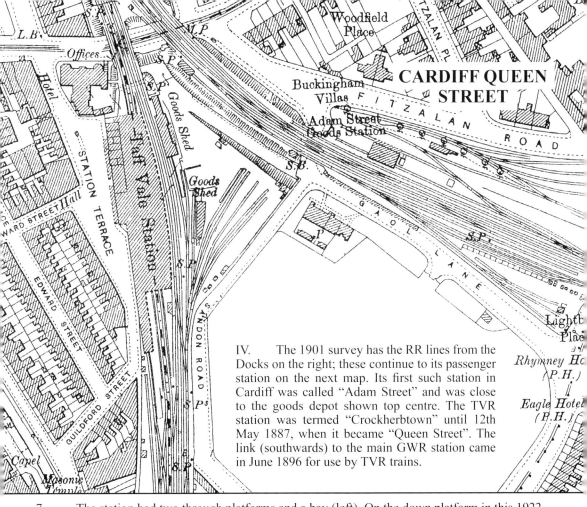

CARDIFF QUEEN STREET

IV.   The 1901 survey has the RR lines from the Docks on the right; these continue to its passenger station on the next map. Its first such station in Cardiff was called "Adam Street" and was close to the goods depot shown top centre. The TVR station was termed "Crockherbtown" until 12th May 1887, when it became "Queen Street". The link (southwards) to the main GWR station came in June 1896 for use by TVR trains.

7.   The station had two through platforms and a bay (left). On the down platform in this 1922 view is the signal box which lasted until 15th April 1928. There were 116 employees here in 1929, when 536,457 tickets were issued, almost the peak year. (M.Whitehouse coll.)

↑ 8. Adam Street goods depot was recorded on 23rd August 1959 and it closed on 2nd May 1966. The RR's first passenger station was adjacent until 1st July 1870. The second one (called "Parade") was a little further north and is described in captions 14 to 17. (M.Hale)

9.　　　No. 6434 stands at the original down platform on 12th July 1958. This had become an island in 1922. A fifth platform followed soon after, on the east side of it. (G.Adams/M.J.Stretton coll.)

10.　　　All five platforms are evident in this northward panorama from August 1963. South Box had 167 levers and was in use from 1928 until 27th June 1966. Beyond it were eight carriage sidings, which were on the site of the goods yard, which had closed on 1st April 1925. (P.J.Garland/R.S.Carpenter)

11.   Junctions north of the station were eliminated on 27th June 1966, but this one is seen a few years after it came into use on 3rd May 1971, after which time only three platforms were in use. The northbound class 116 DMU is viewed from the BR(WR) Divisional Headquarters, Brunel House. A multi-storey car park now occupies the area to the left of the train, which is taking the former RR route. Salisbury Road Goods Depot was between the two routes and it lasted until 27th June 1966. (N.W.Sprinks)

12.	A northward panorama from May 2001 has platform 3 on the right. This was used for the shuttle service to Cardiff Bay. Alterations made in 1990 allowed two trains to use platform 2 simultaneously and made direct access to platform 3 from the north possible. Much of the scaffolding on the AA's Fanum House (left) fell on the track on 13th December 2000, during a storm. Brunel House is on the right. (B.W.L.Brooksbank)

13.	This is the crossover added in 1990, which meant that platform 3 ceased to be a bay. A third track was then provided for Cardiff Bay trains south of the station, plus another crossover. When photographed in 2008, the platform was used every 12 minutes daily by the shuttle train. (H.Ballantyne)

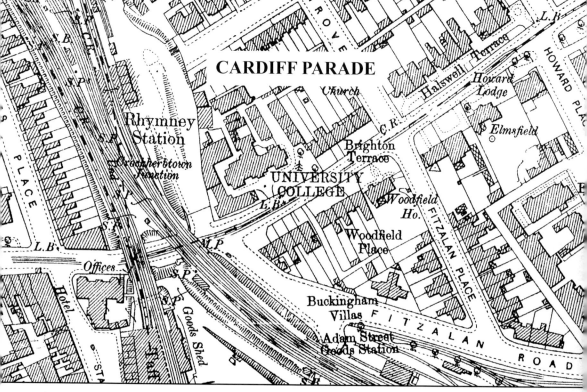

V.   This map continues north from the previous one and has the TVR tracks on the left. It shows that RR trains could not access the TVR. The station was Cardiff (Rhymney) until 1st July 1924 and Cardiff Parade until closure on 15th April 1928.

14.   An up train is seen at the down platform prior to 1917, with no. 31. This was an H class 0-6-0ST from Sharp Stewart in 1872. (P.Q.Treloar coll.)

15.	A northward view from June 1922 has TVR equipment beyond the fence on the left. The entire site would soon be cleared, as the GWR had taken over. There had been 187 employees based here in 1923.
(D.K.Jones coll.)

16.	The east elevation was photographed at the same time and included is the gateway to the short bay platform, which had been added in 1908 to ease evening congestion.
(D.K.Jones coll.)

17.	A view south along the "departure" platform has the main building in the right background. The RR signal box was superseded by Cardiff Queen Street North on 4th March 1928. This had 200 levers and was in use until 20th December 1964.
(Lens of Sutton coll.)

Coryton Branch

HEATH JUNCTION

← VI. The 1956 edition at 1ins to 1 mile has our route vertically on the far right and the junction is just below the two adjacent halts. Cemetery Halt was south thereof, for a brief period. Curving west from them is the former Cardiff Railway branch, which had terminated at Coryton Halt for passengers since 1931. There was some freight passing through the station shown as closed at Tongwynlais, in the 1951-52 period.

18. A DMU from Coryton approaches the junction on 6th August 1963 and passes the 1927 signal box, which had 77 levers, reduced to 27 in June 1966. The train will soon pass Crwys Sidings box, which closed at that time. (G.H.Tilt)

19. A southbound freight was recorded on 24th July 1966 after removal of the sidings, point rodding and most of the signals. A panel in a Portakabin was used after 18th November 1984. The junction was moved 300yds northwards at that time, this releasing land for housing. The branch was entirely single from 1966. (G.H.Tilt)

HEATH LOW LEVEL

CARDIFF RAILWAY

Viaduct

S.P

S.P

Ford

S.P

S.P

Heath Halt

Kennel Cottages

S.B.

VII. The two signal boxes shown on this 1920 map were both closed in 1927. Heath North had opened in 1893 with 18 levers and Heath Sidings West is below it. Off the map was Heath South, which was near the junction. It also closed in 1927.

Heath Halt

S.P.

S.P.

S.B.

Air Shafts.

S.P.

20.   The down platform and waiting room were recorded in about 1920 from the road bridge; the up one is almost under the camera. They were extended in about 1930. (Lens of Sutton coll.)

21.   Residential development followed between the wars and facilities were improved. "Low Level" appeared on the nameboards on 1st July 1924. Only the down platform (right) remained after the singling of the branch. (Stations UK)

22.   Bound for Nantgarw Colliery on 30th May 1952 is 0-6-2T no. 35, an ex-RR class AP from Hudswell Clarke in 1921. The link north was used from 28th August 1951 until 16th June 1952, while connections were altered at the colliery, following its modernisation. The suffix "Halt" was used until 5th May 1969. (S.Rickard/J&J coll.)

TY GLAS

23.   This stop was added on 29th April 1987 and "Pacer" no. 143608 was recorded on 28th October 2008, working the 10.15 Coryton to Radyr "City Line" service. (N.W.Sprinks)

BIRCHGROVE

24.	An eastward view in 1958 presents an open and airy landscape, which is in great contrast to the congested "Tunnel of Trees" so common in the neglected environment of the 21st century. (Stations UK)

25.	A record from July 1976 includes a Pagoda shelter of GWR origin and the main entrance, lower right. This stop had been added by the GWR on 10th June 1929. There was a signal box from 1942 to 1964 to control access to private sidings, some of which served the 1940 ordnance factory. (D.K.Jones)

RHIWBINA

26. No. 5572 heads the 12.45 from Bute Road on 13th August 1958, an autotrain working. The C on the target board indicates the loco as working from Cathays Depot. K was for Dowlais (Cae Harris) and N was for Merthyr.
(S.Rickard/J&J coll.)

27. A view in the other direction, also in 1958, reveals the provision of more substantial shelters, with hipped roofs. The spelling was "Rhubina" until 1916.
(Stations UK)

28. As elsewhere, the down platform was retained and vegetation ran riot. The "Pacer" is the 09.45 Coryton to Radyr on 28th October 2008. Security can be noted on the pole of the security cameras.
(N.W.Sprinks)

WHITCHURCH (GLAM.)

29.   Photographed in June 1922, this was the most substantial station on the route. In the background is the goods shed and the 20-lever signal box. A military hospital nearby generated extra traffic during World War II. Until the service was cut back to Coryton, almost half of the trains terminated here. (D.K.Jones coll.)

VIII. The 1920 survey shows housing development in progress.

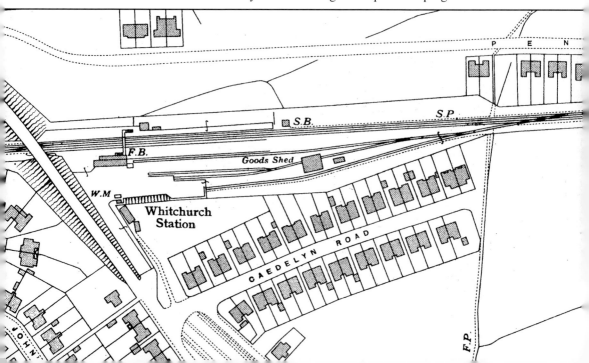

30.   Waiting with the 1.19pm to Cardiff on 12th September 1951 is no. 344, an ex-TVR 0-6-2T. The suffix (Glam.) was used from 1st July 1924. It was (South Glam.) after 1975 and later became (Cardiff). There was a staff of at least five throughout the 1930s, but staffing ceased in June 1964. (H.C.Casserley)

31.   Standing in the rain is an excursion to the seaside at Barry Island on 29th June 1958, when the DMUs were still fairly new. The goods yard closed on 2nd December 1963. (S.Rickard/J&J coll.)

CORYTON

32.   No. 5568 stands on the single line with a three-coach autotrain on 13th May 1954. The terminus was called Coryton Halt until 5th May 1969. The far end of the 1932 little-used loop is beyond the train. The route had been singled west of Whitchurch on 16th May 1928 and the loop lasted until 15th October 1964. (R.S.Carpenter)

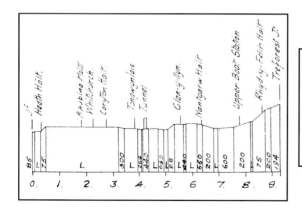

Whitchurch	1923	1929	1930	19
Passenger tickets issued	9242	4297	3673	47
Season tickets issued	266	1062	1347	14
Parcels forwarded	1455	4781	5454	4
General goods forwarded (tons)	391	92	77	8
Coal and coke received (tons)	8234	4599	5972	25
Other minerals received (tons)	8796	1048	1151	15
General goods received (tons)	2234	1751	1281	1'
Trucks of livestock handled	37	3	-	

33.   The buffer stops are close to the bridge in the background. The platform had been west of the bridge until 1931 and passenger trains had continued beyond here to Rhydyfelin Low Level Halt until that time. "Pacer" no. 142073 *Myfanwy* is waiting to return to Radyr at 09.15 on 28th October 2008. The route north had been disused in 1931-51 and closed completely in 1952. (N.W.Sprinks)

In Memoriam

The branch is all that remains of the ambitious Cardiff Railway. It was conceived as a replica of the Barry Railway to link the coal mining area with the ships. Its parents were Lord Bute and his Dock Company, which already had a busy docks railway system. After years of disputes, the northern connection with the TVR was never used regularly and the southern one, between Heath and Bute Docks, remained a dream. Ironically, a railway intended for coal conveyance, evolved to serve local residents exclusively.

HEATH HIGH LEVEL

34.   The halt was opened by the RR in October 1915 to compete with the CR's of 1911, but its elevated position was bad in rough weather. This DMU is bound for Cardiff on 26th April 1960. (S.Rickard/J&J coll.)

➔ 35. The suffix High Level was in use from 1st July 1924. "Pacer" nos. 143624 and 142002 are working the 10.25 Bargoed to Penarth on 28th October 2008. A recent property development is named "Heath Halt Court" and nearby is Heath Halt Road, so the old name lives on. (N.W.Sprinks)

NORTH OF
HEATH HIGH LEVEL

36.   The relationship of the viaduct to the halts is shown on map VII, near picture nos 20-21. A northbound train was recorded in about 1960, with a Vauxhall in the foreground. (S.Rickard/J&J coll.)

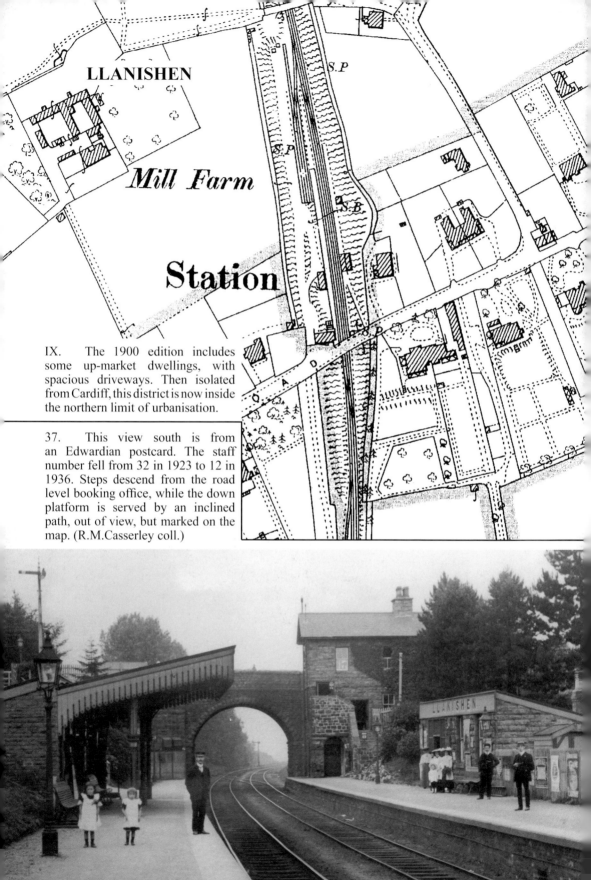

LLANISHEN

Mill Farm

Station

S.P

S.P

S.B

IX.   The 1900 edition includes some up-market dwellings, with spacious driveways. Then isolated from Cardiff, this district is now inside the northern limit of urbanisation.

37.   This view south is from an Edwardian postcard. The staff number fell from 32 in 1923 to 12 in 1936. Steps descend from the road level booking office, while the down platform is served by an inclined path, out of view, but marked on the map. (R.M.Casserley coll.)

38.   An up train calls for mostly women in May 1964. The goods yard (left) closed on 27th June 1966. The signal box (right) was only opened as required. It had 24 levers and closed in about July 1962. The path down to the down platform is on the right of this and the next picture. (S.Rickard/J&J coll.)

39.   The old up platform shelter was still standing on 14th August 2008, as no. 142083 was bound for Tirphil and no. 150237 was destined for Cardiff. The line north of Tirphil was closed for five weeks for engineering work. (H.Ballantyne)

40.   Many sidings were required between the collieries and the docks for holding wagons awaiting ships. No. 40 draws into Cherry Orchard Sidings with empty wagons surplus to requirements at Bargoed, on 11th August 1952. Photographs 40 to 47 are not in geographical order, but the sequence used is intended to clarify the evolution of the area. (S.Rickard/J&J coll.)

Llanishen	1923	1929	1930	1933
Passenger tickets issued	81234	52111	46806	54486
Season tickets issued	634	1042	1185	1047
Parcels forwarded	4677	4749	4723	1442
General goods forwarded (tons)	167	249	201	165
Coal and coke received (tons)	1086	770	781	292
Other minerals received (tons)	6147	1297	1040	1307
General goods received (tons)	727	530	266	254
Trucks of livestock handled	42	33	41	19

41.　　The track on the right of the previous picture was lifted and its bed is on the left of this view in the other direction in 1963. The two signal boxes are seen again, near the bridge. The one near us closed on 10th July 1966; it had 46 levers. Cefn On Halt is beyond the footbridge and not visible. (P.J.Garland/R.S.Carpenter)

42.　　At the south end of Cherry Orchard Sidings were wagon repair shops. Seen again, passing by in May 1952, is no. 35, an ex-RR 0-6-2T built by Hudswell Clarke in 1921. The sidings closed in September 1964, as did the goods yard. (R.C.Riley/Transport Treasury)

LISVANE & THORNHILL

43.   The new station and an extensive car park came into use on 4th November 1985, their location being close to the site of picture 42. The facilities were to replace Cefn On, which had no road access. Much new housing arose at Thornhill. (Lens of Sutton coll.)

44.   To make good shortages of DMUs around the turn of the century, locomotive hauled stock was hired. No. 47777 is seen with the 13.15 Rhymney to Cardiff Central on 15th March 1997. Such operation continued for around ten years, but only at busy times. (N.W.Sprinks)

CEFN ON

45.   Steep paths descended to both platforms, the one on the left being so steep as to terminate with steps. Passing through on 26th June 1954 is 0-6-0PT no. 3753 with the 12.30 Rhymney to Stonefield Junction service. The halt opened in October 1915. (D.K.Jones coll.)

46.	A Cardiff to Sengenhenydd service on 11th August 1956 was hauled by 2-6-2T no. 4589. On the left are the signals for Cherry Orchard Sidings. Originally the spelling was Cefn-Onn and the short platform served a golf course and the public gardens. "Halt" was discontinued in 1969. (S.Rickard/J&J coll.)

47.	The regulars shuffle to their usual boarding point, as the camera approaches on 17th August 1963. They were employees at the shops mentioned in caption 42. Note the improved signal sighting by that time. Closure came on 4th October 1987, but the 1941yd long Caerphilly Tunnel continues to accommodate a busy double track. Water seepage is always a problem and a small roof fall took place in 1947. However, about 60 million gallons of water was piped to Cardiff each year for use by locomotives. (P.J.Garland/R.S.Carpenter)

CAERPHILLY RAILWAY WORKS

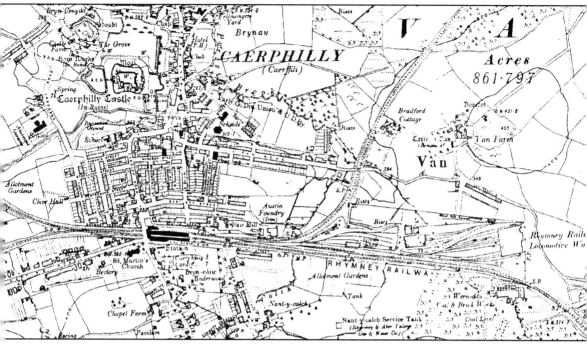

X.   Our route is lower right on this 1922 extract at 6ins to 1 mile. It passes Wern-ddu Brickworks, where sidings are shown. There was a signal box here from 1886 until 1973, when it had a 31-lever frame. The line from here to the lower left curve had existed since 1859. Upper right is the 1864 route to Machen of the B&MR, which we will traverse before looking at the station with picture 65.

48.   The RR's new locomotive works was opened in December 1901 and is the low part on the left. It became the machine shop after the GWR built the lofty extension as an erecting shop in 1926. The large doorway was for a traverser. (GWR)

49.   Wernddu Box and the erecting shop are on the left as 0-6-2T no. 393 approaches Caerphilly Tunnel on 29th August 1952. The other buildings are late GWR additions. A new carriage shop was completed in 1939. (S.Rickard/J&J coll.)

XI.   The locomotive shops are on the right and the smaller buildings on the left were the carriage and wagon works. The survey is from 1920 and part of the goods yard is on the left.

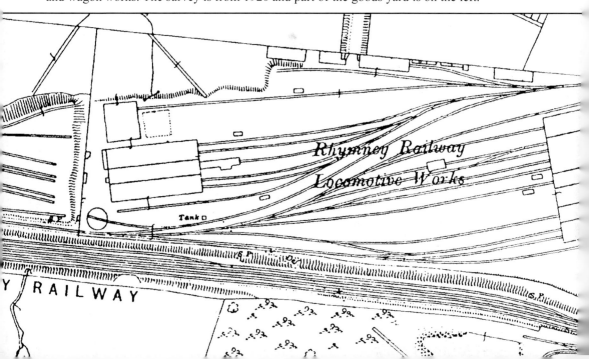

50.   After 1922, the Works became the repair centre for South Wales and received the largest of GWR locos, such as "Castle" 4-6-0s. Above 2-6-2T no. 5527 is one of the girders for the 30-ton capacity travelling crane. Rotting doors and old line shafting begin to date the premises. (D.K.Jones coll.)

51.   Much of the work had to be undertaken outdoors, despite all the additions and extensions. No. 2196 *Gwendraeth* had another four years life ahead of her when photographed on 6th July 1952. (B.K.B.Green/Initial Photographics)

52.   The 10-coach platform for workers was used by members of the Gloucester Railway Society during a visit on 12th May 1956. No. 391 was an ex-TVR 0-6-2T. At the end of the RR in 1922, it had 99 0-6-2Ts, 22 0-6-0Ts and two 2-4-2Ts. (D.K.Jones coll.)

53.   Our last photograph of the Works is from 1951 and features the final extensions. Recently outshopped and in pristine condition is 0-6-2T no. 5686; the 5600 class was introduced in 1924. The works closed on 28th June 1963, with the loss of 443 jobs. The area became an industrial estate. (J.H.Bramley/D.H.Mitchell)

CAERPHILLY TAR WORKS

54.   The premises were established by Powell Duffryn. Tar was a byproduct of the manufacture of town gas from coal and most arrived here by rail from the gasworks of the area. Much of it went out for use as a roadstone binder before the widespread use of bitumen. Shunting the tankers in December 1956 is 0-6-0T no. 2034, which has recently been purchased from BR. (P.Q.Treloar)

XII. Part of the Tar Works appeared on the 1939 edition.

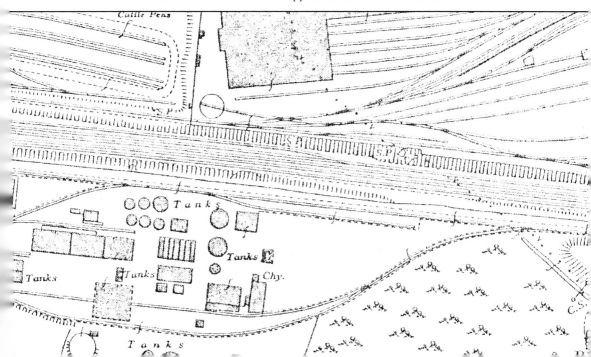

55.	Out of use on 28th August 1960, was Hawthorn Leslie 0-4-0ST *Lucifer* of 1916. Drums of tar went away to the building and manufacturing industries. Thomas Ness Works was distilling tar from 1939 until 1986. It was demolished, but the polluted land was unusable. (M.Dart/Transport Treasury)

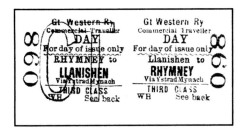

CAERPHILLY RAILWAY SOCIETY

The CRS took over the site from the Great Western Society South Wales Group who in turn had taken over the South Wales Switchgear Railway Society who had the care of ex-TVR 0-6-2T No. 28.

56.   The group obtained use of some ¼ mile of track on the north side of the former Works site in about 1973. Two photographs from 28th June 1981 show part of the demonstration line and include Robert Stephenson & Hawthorn no. 7705 of 1952. (T.Heavyside)

57.   On the right is Andrew Barclay no. 2201 of 1945, named *Victory* and left is a former RR somersault signal. The signal box had been on the B&MR at Rhiwderin. The site was vacated in 1996 and the collection dispersed, mainly to the Gwili Railway near Carmarthen. (T.Heavyside)

Caerphilly to Machen

GWERNYDOMEN HALT

XIII.   Seen on the 1ins to 1 mile map of 1954, the route runs eastwards from Caerphilly and is seen to split into two single lines east of the first halt. The lower one is the original of 1864 and the other was added in 1891. The line with + and - is the then national boundary and it generally followed the River Rhymney. Rhos Llantwit Colliery had a siding from 1875 to 1912. It was north of Van.

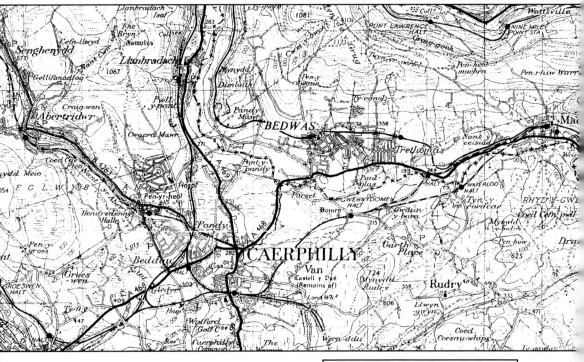

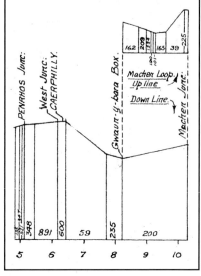

58. The halt was in use from 1st April 1908 until 17th September 1956 and this is the south side of the bridge in the following year. Gwain y Bara Sidings were near the divergence of the lines from 1900 until 1956. (R.M.Casserley coll.)

59. Another 1957 photograph records the other "platform". The lantern has been left open - the guard was provided with a stepping block to enable him to change the oil lamps. (S.Rickard/J&J coll.)

60. The dates for this stopping place are as shown in caption 58. No. 4130 was running through with a Caerphilly-Newport service on 30th August 1956. This was termed the down line.
(S.C.L.Phillips/
D.J.Jones coll.)

61. The train has stopped with its ends in different countries on 11th July 1959. Few places had trains stopping in one direction only - the station for emigrants near Southampton was another example.
(G.Adams/
M.J.Stretton coll.)

62.   This view features 0-6-0PT no. 6411 and a sign proclaiming the location as "Waterloo". This was the other unidirectional platform - both had the same dates. West of here was Waterloo Tinplate Works Siding from 1902. It was used by the Admiralty from 1942 until closure in 1952. (G.Daniels/R.M.Casserley coll.)

WHITE HART HALT

63.   This was a balanced stop, but received only down trains. The up platform was at a high
level, on the steeper gradient of the 1864 line. The halts opened on 12th May 1947 and closed on
30th June 1952, the year of the photograph. Upper left is the line which features in our *Brecon to
Newport* album. A siding from the up line west of here served Pentwyn Colliery, Cae Quarry and
Machen Black Vein Pit between 1901 and 1937. (LGRP/NRM)

Gt Western Ry		Gt Western Ry
Caerphilly		Caerphilly
	TO	
	RHYDYFELIN HALT H.L.	
	THIRD CLASS	
8½d P	Fare	8½d P
RhydyfelinHaltH.L		RhydyfelinHaltH.L
FOR CONDITIONS SEE BACK.		W.D

671   671

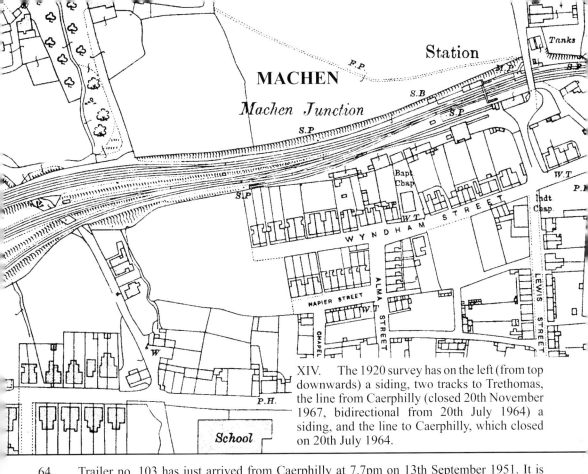

MACHEN

Machen Junction

Station

XIV. The 1920 survey has on the left (from top downwards) a siding, two tracks to Trethomas, the line from Caerphilly (closed 20th November 1967, bidirectional from 20th July 1964) a siding, and the line to Caerphilly, which closed on 20th July 1964.

64. Trailer no. 103 has just arrived from Caerphilly at 7.7pm on 13th September 1951. It is being propelled over the crossover before being run round by 0-6-2T no. 351. They will depart for Pontypridd at 7.20, as seen in picture no. 104 in our *Brecon to Newport* album. (H.C.Casserley)

CAERPHILLY

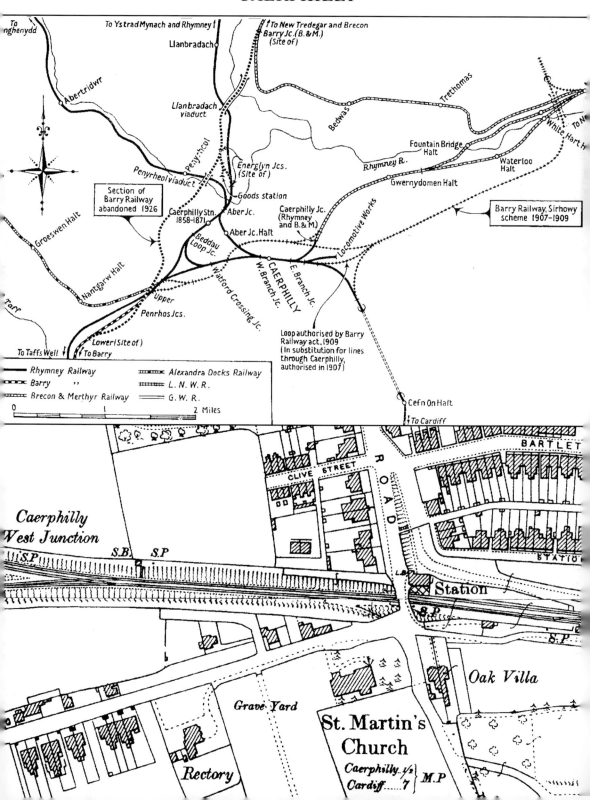

To nghenydd

To Ystrad Mynach and Rhymney

Llanbradach

To New Tredegar and Brecon
Barry Jc. (B. & M.)
(Site of)

Abertridwr

Llanbradach
viaduct

Trethomas

Bedwas

Pen-y-heol

Penyrheol viaduct

Energlyn Jcs.
(Site of)

Fountain Bridge
Halt

Rhymney R.

Waterloo
Halt

Goods station

White Hart h

To Ne

Section of
Barry Railway
abandoned 1926

Gwernydomen Halt

Caerphilly Stn.
1858-1871

Aber Jc.

Caerphilly Jc.
(Rhymney
and B. & M.)

Barry Railway, Sirhowy
scheme 1907-1909

Groeswen Halt

Aber Jc. Halt

Beddau
Loop Jc.

Locomotive Works

Nantgarw Halt

Watford Crossing Jc.

CAERPHILLY

W. Branch Jc.

E. Branch Jc.

Taff

Upper
Penrhos Jcs.

Loop authorised by Barry
Railway act. 1909
(In substitution for lines
through Caerphilly,
authorised in 1907)

To Taffs Well

Lower (Site of)

To Barry

Cefn On Halt

To Cardiff

—— Rhymney Railway   ┅┅┅ Alexandra Docks Railway
╍╍╍ Barry   "   ┼┼┼┼ L. N. W. R.
╌╌╌ Brecon & Merthyr Railway ═══ G. W. R.

0 .... 1 .... 2 Miles

Caerphilly
West Junction

CLIVE STREET

ROAD

BARTLET

S.P

S.B.

S.P

STATION

Station

S.P

S.P

Oak Villa

Grave Yard

St. Martin's
Church

Rectory

Caerphilly ½
Cardiff 7

M.P

← XV. Origin of the railways in the area and their relationship to the Rhymney River. (Railway Magazine)

↙ XVI. To confirm the location of the 1898 edition, one can refer back to the map near picture 48. The private sidings lead from the small goods yard. A much larger one was laid further east in 1913, when the signal boxes shown were replaced.

65. This postcard features the first station on the second site, as shown on the map. There was access from Cardiff Road direct into the first floor and the dock location is revealed by the position of the cattle wagon. The station opened on 1st April 1871.
(Lens of Sutton coll.)

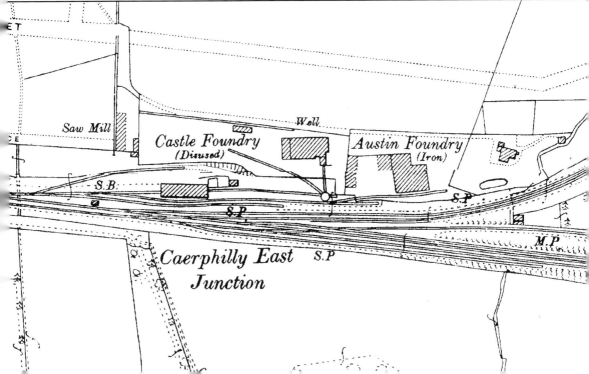

66.   During the total rebuild of 1913, a new and longer road bridge was built, this allowing two extra through lines to be laid, as seen in 1922. A bay for Machen line trains was provided on the right. The footbridge was for the public path shown at ground level on the map. (D.K.Jones coll.)

67.   A view from about 1935 includes all five platforms, together with West Box beyond the bridge. Its 45-lever frame was in use until 1968. (Stations UK)

68.   A workmans train stands close to 0-6-2T no. 377 on 29th August 1952, its destination being the Works in the distance. The gable end of the goods shed is evident to the right of East Box, which contained 132 levers. (S.Rickard/J&J coll.)

69.   The 1913 bridge and offices are featured as 2-6-2T no. 4589 departs with the Senghenydd autotrain on 13th August 1954. The building survives and is in commercial use. (S.Rickard/J&J coll.)

← 70. No. 9401 is destined for Aber Junction with freight from Radyr on 26th April 1960. It is passing behind East Box, which closed on 20th July 1964. The bay platform is in the foreground. (S.Rickard/J&J coll.)

← 71. Major alterations took place in 1973, these involving the loss of the three platforms added in 1913 and their replacement by a bus station. A new entrance was built between it and the down platform. We see the 17.20 Rhymney to Penarth on 28th June 1981. (T.Heavyside)

72. A photograph from 14th October 1999 reveals improvements at the bus station, but the covered footbridge evident in the previous picture had been replaced by an open one. No. 31459 was hauling the 13.16 Bargoed to Cardiff Central, an extra train in connection with a sporting event in that city. Loco hauled passenger trains were a feature on the Rhymney line for a few years, due to a DMU shortage. They generally ran as 6-coach sets of BR Mk II stock, at morning and evening peaks. The later sets looked quite smart in an overall maroon livery. Loco haulage ceased in December 2006. (D.H.Mitchell)

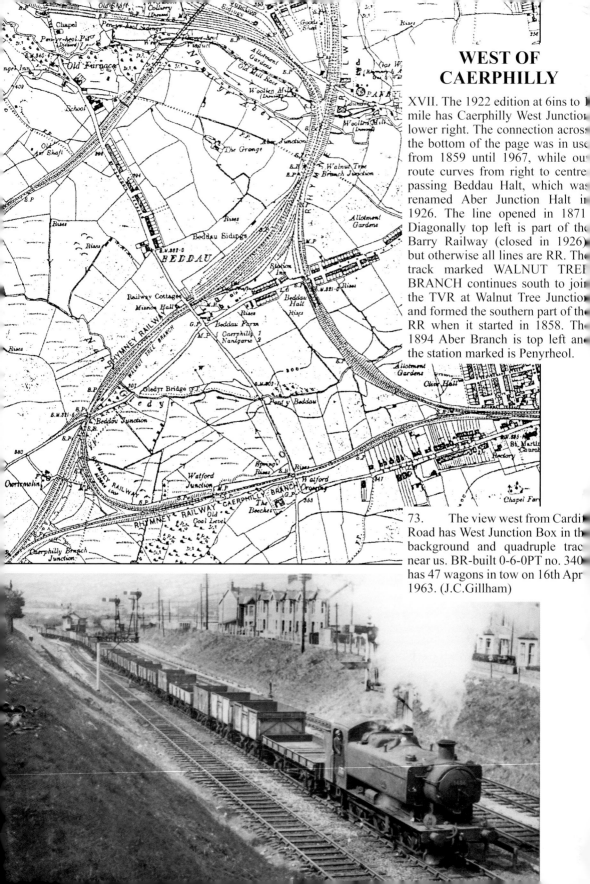

WEST OF CAERPHILLY

XVII. The 1922 edition at 6ins to 1 mile has Caerphilly West Junction lower right. The connection across the bottom of the page was in use from 1859 until 1967, while our route curves from right to centre passing Beddau Halt, which was renamed Aber Junction Halt in 1926. The line opened in 1871. Diagonally top left is part of the Barry Railway (closed in 1926) but otherwise all lines are RR. The track marked WALNUT TREE BRANCH continues south to join the TVR at Walnut Tree Junction and formed the southern part of the RR when it started in 1858. The 1894 Aber Branch is top left and the station marked is Penyrheol.

73.   The view west from Cardiff Road has West Junction Box in the background and quadruple track near us. BR-built 0-6-0PT no. 3405 has 47 wagons in tow on 16th April 1963. (J.C.Gillham)

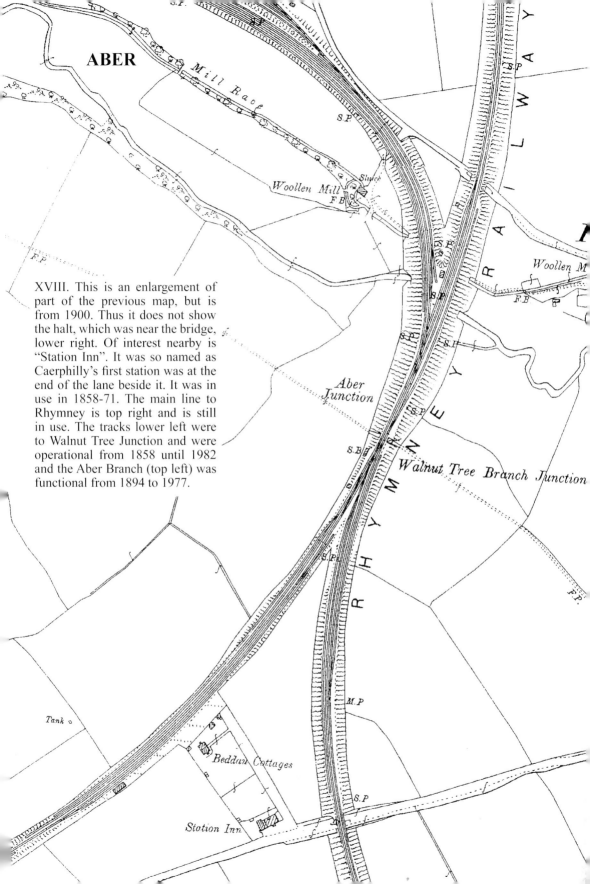

ABER

Mill Race

Woollen Mill
F.B.

Woollen M
F.B.

Aber Junction

XVIII. This is an enlargement of part of the previous map, but is from 1900. Thus it does not show the halt, which was near the bridge, lower right. Of interest nearby is "Station Inn". It was so named as Caerphilly's first station was at the end of the lane beside it. It was in use in 1858-71. The main line to Rhymney is top right and is still in use. The tracks lower left were to Walnut Tree Junction and were operational from 1858 until 1982 and the Aber Branch (top left) was functional from 1894 to 1977.

S.B.

Walnut Tree Branch Junction

Tank

M.P.

Beddau Cottages

S.P.

Station Inn

74.   Opened on 1st April 1908 as Beddau Halt, it became Aber Junction Halt on 17th September 1926. It is seen from the north not long before it became Aber Halt on 6th May 1968. "Halt" was dropped a year later and it was still open after more than 40 years. (Lens of Sutton coll.)

75.   Aber Junction Box was recorded in August 1963. Its 107 lever frame was in use from March 1953 until May 1987. There are running lines behind it. The route northwards was doubled in 1872. (P.J.Garland/R.S.Carpenter)

76.   Moving level with the signal box, we see the Aber Branch curving left from the Rhymney main line. All has now gone and houses cover the area each side of the tracks. (P.J.Garland/R.S.Carpenter)

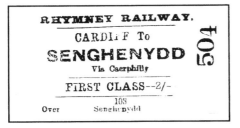

Aber Branch
PENYRHEOL HALT

XIX.   The 1900 edition shows the goods yard to be at a lower level than the running line. The yard closed on 16th July 1957. The name is usually spoken as Pen-er-reel.

← 77. This eastward view is from July 1958 and has Aber Junction signals in the distance. Passenger service ceased when the branch closed. (H.C.Casserley)

78. We look in the other direction in August 1963, ten years after it had been designated a halt and staffing ceased. There had been eight men in 1923, this reducing to 4 by 1930. (P.J.Garland/R.S.Carpenter)

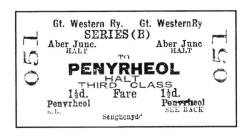

Gt. Western Ry.   Gt. WesternRy
SERIES (B)
Aber Junc.   Aber Junc
HALT   HALT
TO
PENYRHEOL
HALT
THIRD   CLASS
1¼d.   Fare   1¼d.
Penyrheol   Penyrheol
L.E.   SEE BACK
Senghenyd⁴

051   051

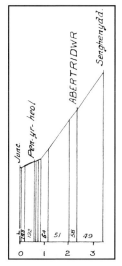

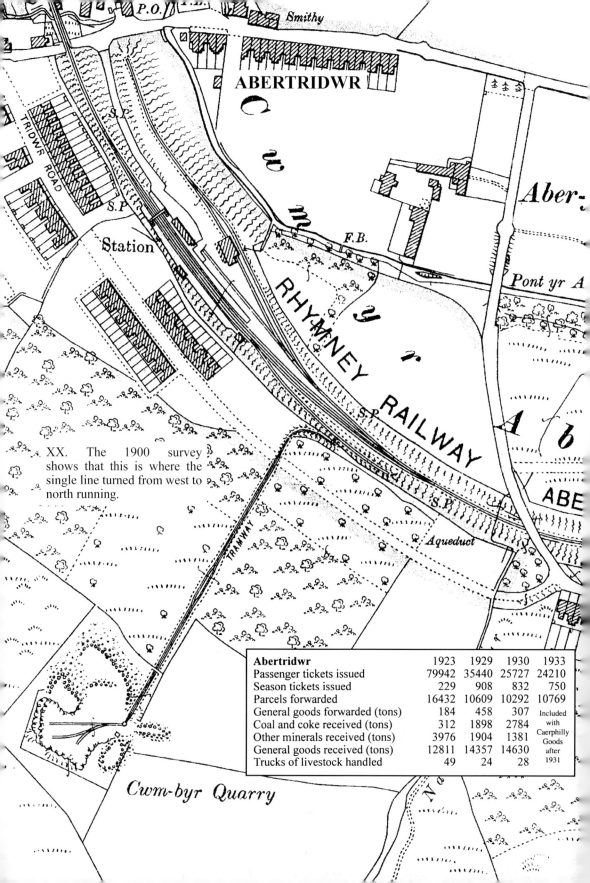

P.O.

Smithy

ABERTRIDWR

Aber-

S.P.

TRIDWR ROAD

S.P.

Station

F.B.

Pont yr A

RHYMNEY RAILWAY

S.P.

A b

XX. The 1900 survey shows that this is where the single line turned from west to north running.

S.P.

ABE

TRAMWAY

Aqueduct

Abertridwr	1923	1929	1930	1933
Passenger tickets issued	79942	35440	25727	24210
Season tickets issued	229	908	832	750
Parcels forwarded	16432	10609	10292	10769
General goods forwarded (tons)	184	458	307	Included with Caerphilly Goods after 1931
Coal and coke received (tons)	312	1898	2784	
Other minerals received (tons)	3976	1904	1381	
General goods received (tons)	12811	14357	14630	
Trucks of livestock handled	49	24	28	

Cwm-byr Quarry

79.   The station had been called simply "Aber" until 26th June 1899. This view is up the valley at about that time. The manning level dropped from ten in 1923 to seven in 1938. (Lens of Sutton coll.)

80.   This panorama is from August 1963 and includes the goods yard, which closed on 1st March 1965. The quarry siding remains on the left. The massive Windsor Colliery is in the background. (P.J.Garland/R.S.Carpenter)

WINDSOR
COLLIERY HALT

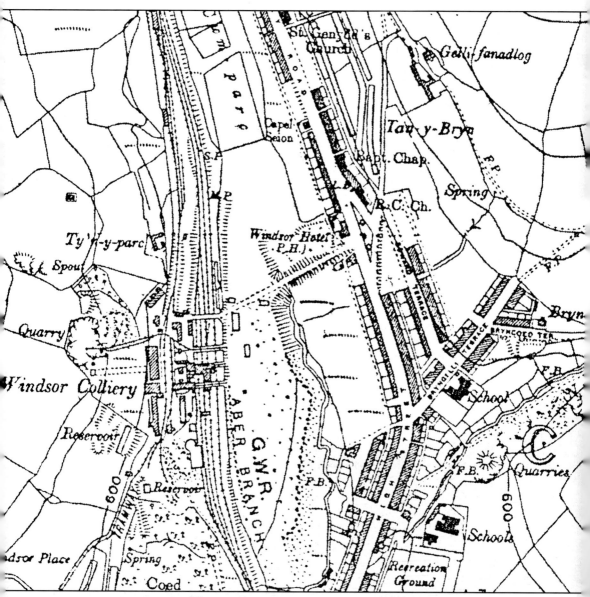

XXI. The 1947 survey is at 3ins to 1 mile. The colliery was employing 2396 men in 1923.

81.   The landscape becomes barren as we approach 600ft above sea level in August 1963 on the steep climb up the valley. The mine was connected underground to Nantgarw Colliery in 1977, distance being 2½ miles, and coal trains on the branch were thus withdrawn. (P.J.Garland/R.S.Carpenter)

82.   Windsor Colliery was opened in about 1900 by the colliery company of the same name. It later became part of the Powell Duffryn group and passed to the National Coal Board in 1947. An early record reveals the advanced loading facilities provided. Colliery closure came on 6th November 1986. Insoles became one of the major coal shippers at Cardiff Docks, having started as colliery owners in the Rhondda in the 19th century. James and Frederick Insole had been colliery owners. (www.oldphotos.com)

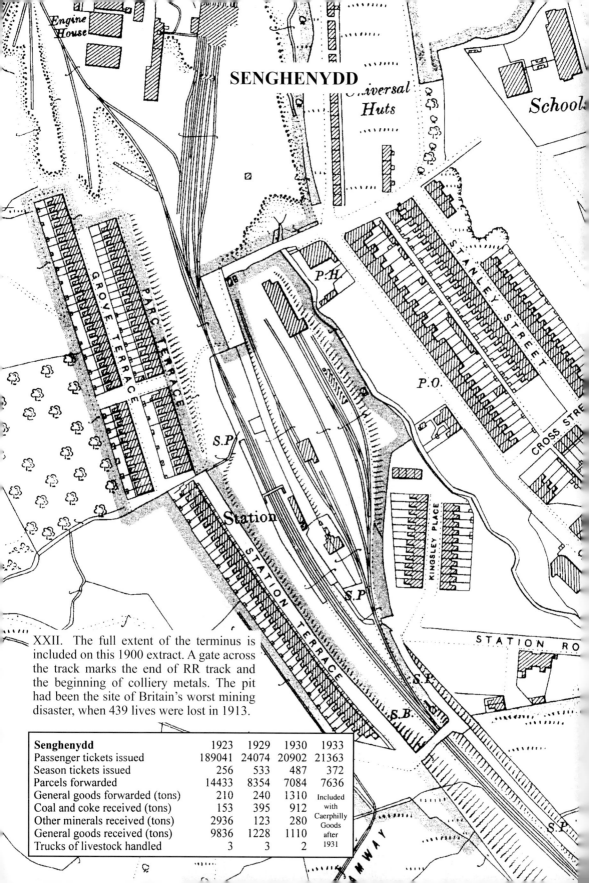

SENGHENYDD

Engine House

Universal Huts

School

P.H.

P.O.

GROVE TERRACE

PARC TERRACE

S.P.

Station

STATION TERRACE

STANLEY STREET

CROSS STRE

KINGSLEY PLACE

S.P.

STATION RO

S.P.

S.B.

AMWAY

S.P.

XXII. The full extent of the terminus is included on this 1900 extract. A gate across the track marks the end of RR track and the beginning of colliery metals. The pit had been the site of Britain's worst mining disaster, when 439 lives were lost in 1913.

Senghenydd	1923	1929	1930	1933
Passenger tickets issued	189041	24074	20902	21363
Season tickets issued	256	533	487	372
Parcels forwarded	14433	8354	7084	7636
General goods forwarded (tons)	210	240	1310	Included
Coal and coke received (tons)	153	395	912	with
Other minerals received (tons)	2936	123	280	Caerphilly
General goods received (tons)	9836	1228	1110	Goods
Trucks of livestock handled	3	3	2	after 1931

83. An observer stands with his portmanteau between his feet as J class 0-6-0ST no. 53 waits to depart south. It was one of a batch built by Sharp Stewart in 1884 for the RR. There were 36 employees here in 1923, but only eight in the late 1930s. (P.Q.Treloar coll.)

84. Resting after arrival with an autotrain sometime in the 1950s is 2-6-2T no. 5572. The up platform had seldom been used. (Lens of Sutton coll.)

85. Universal Collieries pit is in the distance and the site of the engine shed is on the right. It was in use until 23rd May 1931. The photograph is from August 1960 and it includes the water tank, but the colliery connection had gone. There had been two mines; one closed in 1930 and the other in 1961. (M.Dart/ Transport Treasury)

86.   This southward 1963 shot is from the access path, which curves behind the bush and then passes under the line curving to the goods yard. (P.J.Garland/R.S.Carpenter)

87.   On the right is the goods yard, which closed on 2nd July 1962 and is rather overgrown in this undated picture. The figures are above the subway. The area is now covered by houses. (LGRP)

88.   The 1.30pm departure is seen on 28th May 1964, two weeks before service ceased. The redundant loop had been lifted, as coal trains would never come this far north again. (J.C.Gillham)

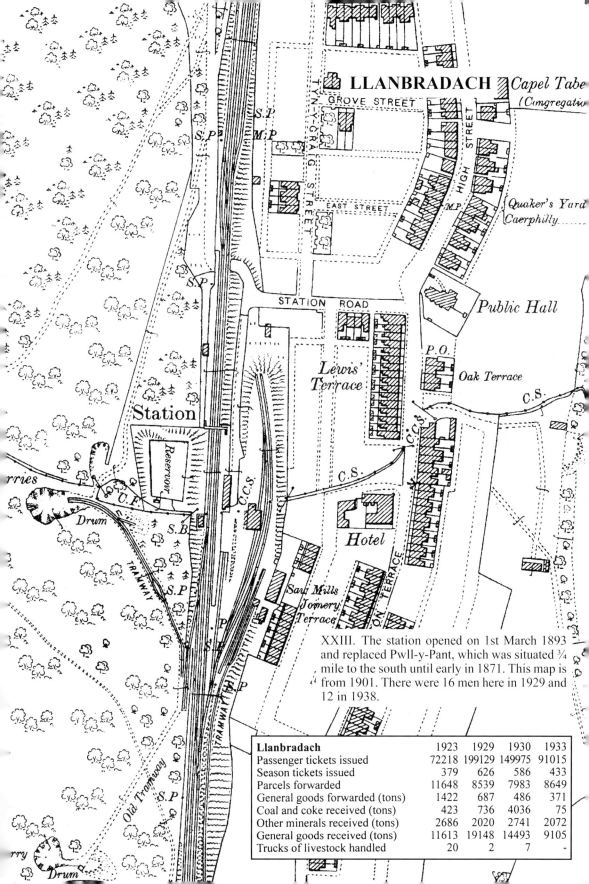

LLANBRADACH *Capel Tabe*
(Congregati

GROVE STREET

TYN-Y-GRAIG STREET

EAST STREET

HIGH STREET

Quaker's Yard
Caerphilly

S.P
M.P

S.P
S.P

M.P

S.P

STATION ROAD

Public Hall

P.O.

Oak Terrace

C.S.

Lewis'
Terrace

C.C.S.

C.S.

Station

Reservoir

C.F.

Drum

S.B.

C.C.S.

C.S.

Hotel

TRAMWAY

S.P

S.P

Saw Mills
Joinery
Terrace

ON TERRACE

rries

P

S

Old Tramway

S.P

rry
Drum

XXIII. The station opened on 1st March 1893
and replaced Pwll-y-Pant, which was situated ¾
mile to the south until early in 1871. This map is
from 1901. There were 16 men here in 1929 and
12 in 1938.

Llanbradach	1923	1929	1930	1933
Passenger tickets issued	72218	199129	149975	91015
Season tickets issued	379	626	586	433
Parcels forwarded	11648	8539	7983	8649
General goods forwarded (tons)	1422	687	486	371
Coal and coke received (tons)	423	736	4036	75
Other minerals received (tons)	2686	2020	2741	2072
General goods received (tons)	11613	19148	14493	9105
Trucks of livestock handled	20	2	7	-

89.   We continue our journey on the former RR main line and look north in August 1963 at the goods yard, which closed on 5th April 1964. The signal box had 86 levers and was in use from 1916 until 8th July 1970.
(P.J.Garland/
R.S.Carpenter)

90.   Llanbradach Colliery is in the background of this and the previous photograph. It was sunk in 1885 and was in production until the end of 1961, the buildings being demolished in 1965. No. 5687 is running between the colliery lines with freight from Bargoed on 27th April 1957.
(S.Rickard/J&J coll.)

91.   As elsewhere on the RR, the platforms were staggered. This was a safety measure before the provision of footbridges. This southward view is from July 1984, by which time housing covered most former railway land.
(D.K.Jones coll.)

YSTRAD MYNACH

Nant

North Junction

Old Quarry

-ryn-mynach

F.P.

Station Terrace

S.P.

S.P.

F.P.

S.B.

S.P.

S.P.

M.P.

M.P.

F.P.

F.P.

Heol-y-cawl

Ystrad-mynach Station

S.P.

F.P.

...EY RAILWAY

d

l

XXIV. The 1900 survey has our route from lower left to top left, the RR main line to Rhymney being top right. The river passes under it. The name is usually said as Us-trud-mun-uck.

92. We have a southward vista from the footbridge joining the main line platforms. The map does not include the bridge or the sidings, only a loop line. The date is 10th July 1958 and no. 5630 is moving the stock of the 4.15pm from Cae Harris, before running round it. (H.C.Casserley)

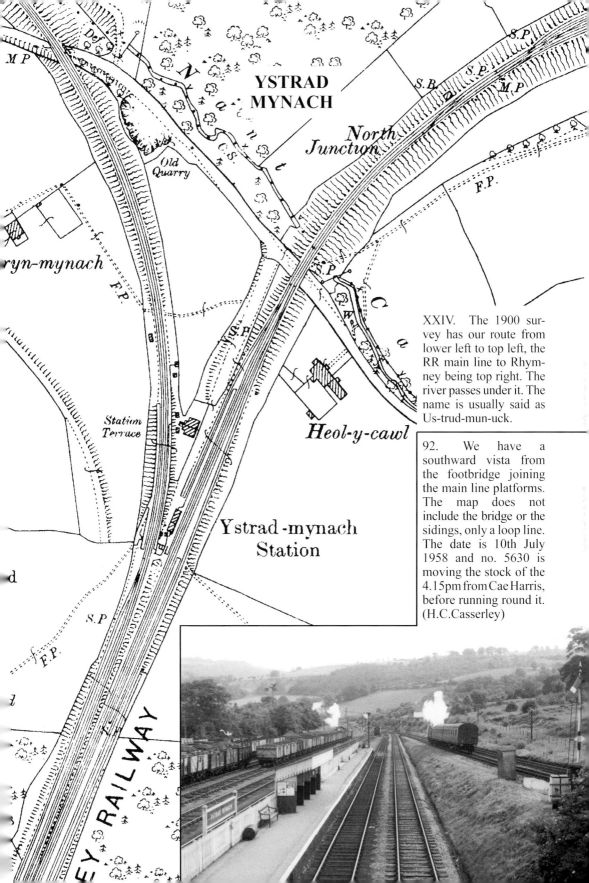

93. The north end of the branch platforms were photographed on the same day. There had been a staff of approaching 30 twenty years earlier, although only a single siding was provided for goods. It was to the right of the cottage on the right and was not used after 20th September 1965. (H.C.Casserley)

94. A branch train stands in the platform on the left, while we look at the main line north, in August 1963. South Box was behind the camera and its 46-lever frame was still in use in 2008. North Box (47 levers) had closed on 19th September 1976. South is illustrated on the back cover. (P.J.Garland/R.S.Carpenter)

95. Viewed from the site of the branch up platform is no. 37287 with a ballast train in the Summer of 1980. The shelter on the remaining down platform is on the left. (P.Jones)

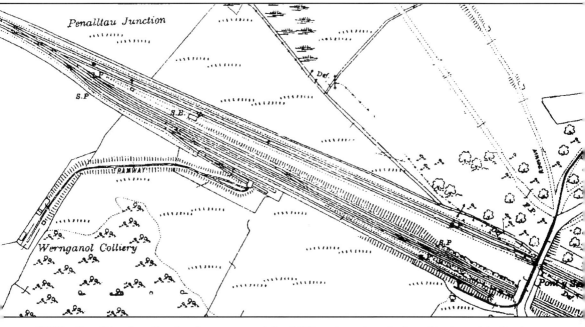

XXV.   Penalltau Junction is where we meet the 1858 east-west route from Pontypool to Quakers Yard. This 1921 map at 17ins to 1 mile includes the siding and tramway to Wernagol Colliery, which saw traffic in the 1911-40 period. It diverges from the lower tracks, which form the 1871 route from Ystrad Mynach. This was doubled in about 1900.

96.   Penalltau Junction Box was the third at this location and served from 1899 until 15th June 1964, having had a 48-lever frame supplied in 1955. The line to Pontypool is to the left of it and the Ystrad Mynach tracks descend in front of it in this 1963 picture. (M.Hale)

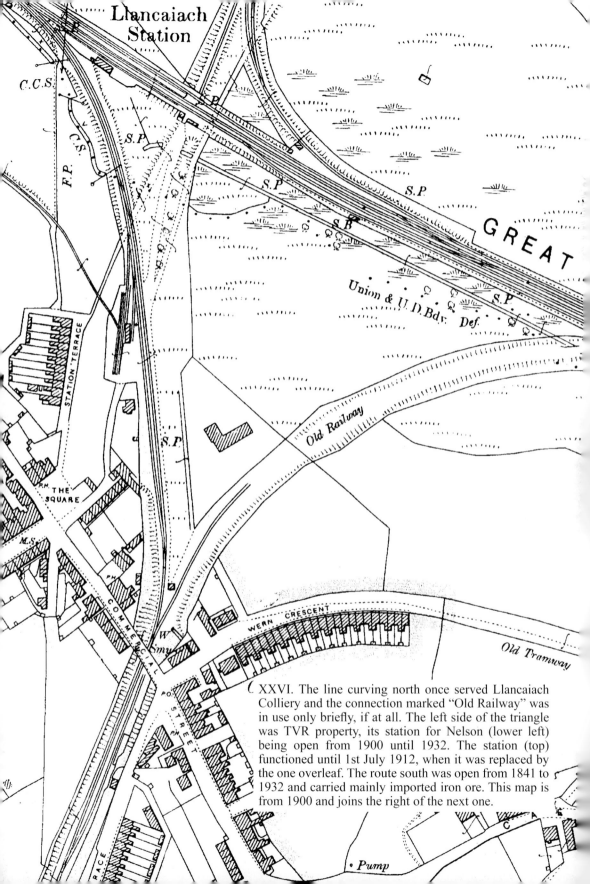

Llancaiach
Station

C.C.S.

F.P.

S.P.

S.P.

STATION TERRACE

P.H. THE
SQUARE

M.S.

COMMERCIAL

S.P.

S.P.

S.P.

S.B.

Union & U.D.Bdy.   Def.

G R E A T

Old Railway

WERN   CRESCENT

Old Tramway

W   Smy.

P.O.

STREET

RACE

XXVI. The line curving north once served Llancaiach
Colliery and the connection marked "Old Railway" was
in use only briefly, if at all. The left side of the triangle
was TVR property, its station for Nelson (lower left)
being open from 1900 until 1932. The station (top)
functioned until 1st July 1912, when it was replaced by
the one overleaf. The route south was open from 1841 to
1932 and carried mainly imported iron ore. This map is
from 1900 and joins the right of the next one.

Pump

NELSON & LLANCAIACH

XXVII.   The 1912 station and layout is seen on the 1920 edition, scaled at 20ins to 1 mile. Our journey will continue on the two lines on the right of those top left.

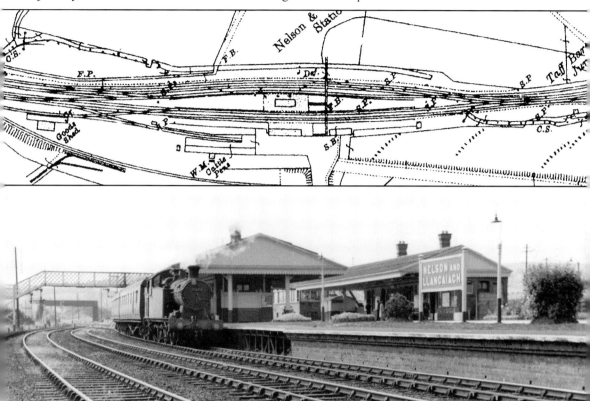

97.   We look south at the island platform on 25th July 1958, as 0-6-2T no. 5671 waits with a train for Dowlais (Cae Harris). On the left are two through lines for freight. (G.Adams/M.J.Stretton coll.)

98.   No. 4688 approaches the station from the east in July 1963. It had a choice of three routes, as revealed by the signals in the distance. (D.K.Jones coll.)

99.   Bound for Neath on 2nd May 1964 is 0-6-0PT no. 8445. The footbridge was also for public use; it ends in a field on the left. (A.M.Davies)

Other views of this station can be found in our *Pontypool to Mountain Ash* album in pictures 76 to 87.

100.   The signal box is included in this view from 28th December 1963. It was in use from 1912 until 10th September 1968 and had a new frame of 94 levers fitted in 1957. Waiting with the branch train is 0-6-2T no. 6612. (M.J.Stretton coll.)

101.   A westward panorama from the footbridge featured in picture 97 has no. 37218 arriving on 30th June 1981, bound for Dowlais (Cae Harris). The "holy" wagons served as barriers, which gave good visibility from the rear cab windows. Nos 37210 and 37255 are waiting with a Merry-go-round coal train from Taff Merthyr and Trelewis, a route which closed in 1996. (T.Heavyside)

TRELEWIS PLATFORM

102.   A 1958 record features the well maintained track northwards and one of the two inclined paths to the platforms. There were many dwellings nearby. The stop came into use on 10th July 1911. (Stations UK)

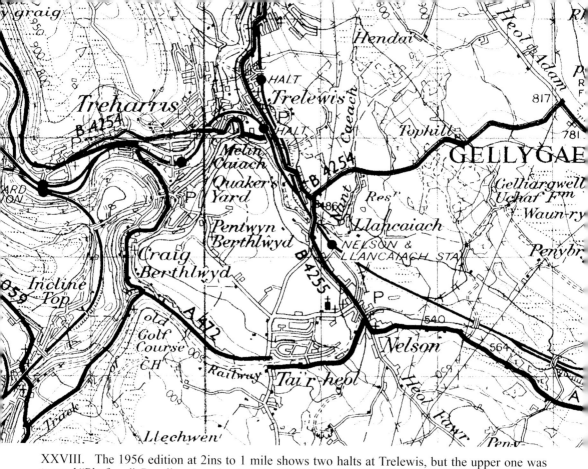

XXVIII.　The 1956 edition at 2ins to 1 mile shows two halts at Trelewis, but the upper one was termed "Platform". Penalltau Junction is on the right and the two stations of Quaker's Yard Junction are on the left. We travel north.

TAFF MERTHYR COLLIERY HALT

103.　　A northward view from August 1963 includes the colliery and the up line, which had not been used since July 1957. It was closed earlier (December 1952 to June 1954) as far as Bedlinog. (P.J.Garland/R.S.Carpenter)

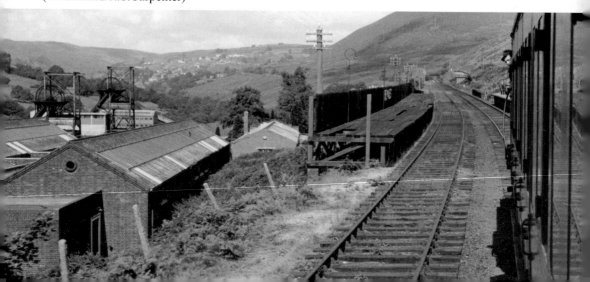

BEDLINOG

104. The goods shed is central in this view of one of the staff; there were ten more in 1903, 21 in 1923 and 10 in 1934. Bedlinog Colliers Platform was in use in 1897-1915 and 1938-54 approximately and was to the north of the station. (Lens of Sutton coll.)

105. Seen on 26th September 1960 is the southern limit of the capacious goods yard, which was open until 7th October 1963. It was in two parts - this is the southern section. (H.C.Casserley)

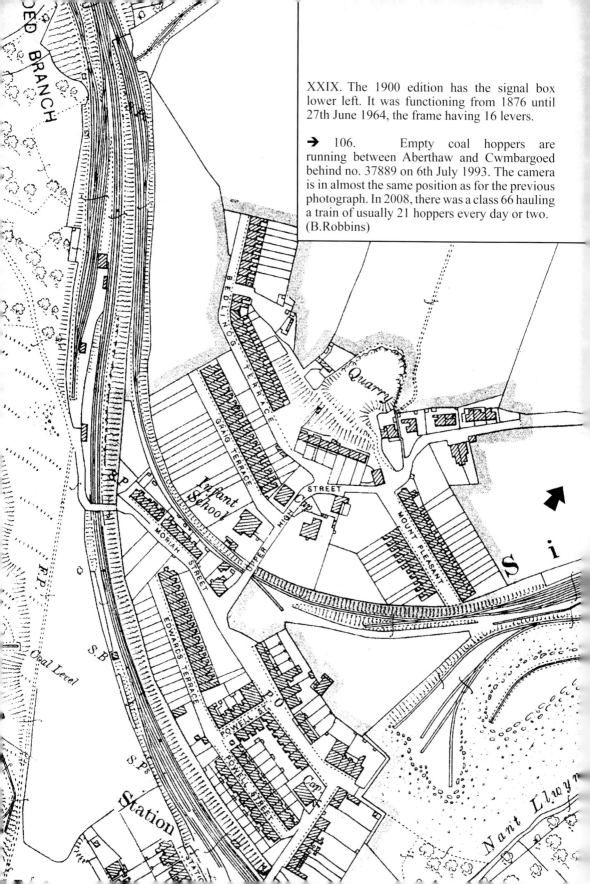

XXIX. The 1900 edition has the signal box lower left. It was functioning from 1876 until 27th June 1964, the frame having 16 levers.

→ 106. Empty coal hoppers are running between Aberthaw and Cwmbargoed behind no. 37889 on 6th July 1993. The camera is in almost the same position as for the previous photograph. In 2008, there was a class 66 hauling a train of usually 21 hoppers every day or two. (B.Robbins)

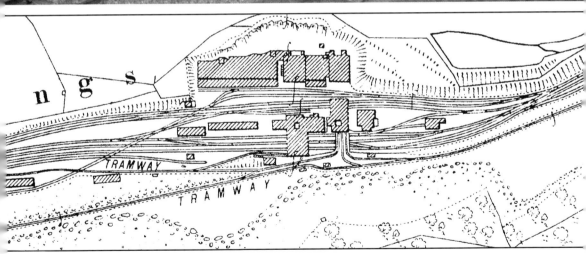

edlinog	1903	1913	1923	1933
Passenger tickets issued	40488	81665	73446	103388
Season tickets issued	*	*	95	38
Parcels forwarded	3909	8760	6265	8628
General goods forwarded (tons)	22	186	339	25
Coal and coke received (tons)	118	258	33	29
Other minerals received (tons)	1050	1950	871	179
General goods received (tons)	606	1367	7003	523
Trucks of livestock handled	9	3	-	-

Cwm Bargoed	1903	1913	1923	1933
Passenger tickets issued	13534	13057	10040	8635
Season tickets issued	*	*	13	5
Parcels forwarded	159	197	151	97
General goods forwarded (tons)	7	43	732	51
Other minerals received (tons)	181	118	330	-
General goods received (tons)	431	436	6627	1483
Trucks of livestock handled	28	20	14	11

CWMBARGOED

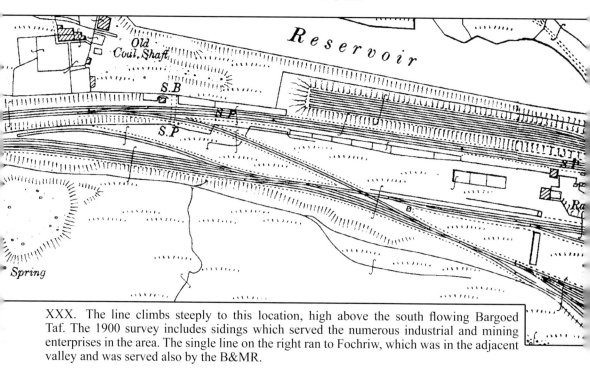

XXX. The line climbs steeply to this location, high above the south flowing Bargoed Taf. The 1900 survey includes sidings which served the numerous industrial and mining enterprises in the area. The single line on the right ran to Fochriw, which was in the adjacent valley and was served also by the B&MR.

XXXI. The 1954 edition at 1 ins to 1 mile has Cwmbargoed right of centre and shows industrial lines linking the stations at Dowlais. Fochriw is lower right and is on the former B&MR featured in *Brecon to Newport*. The route across the map is in *Abergavenny to Merthyr*.

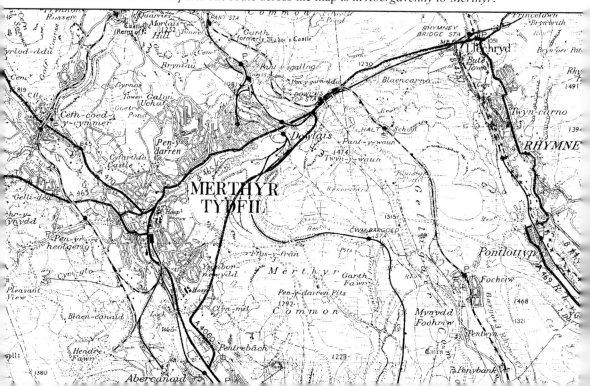

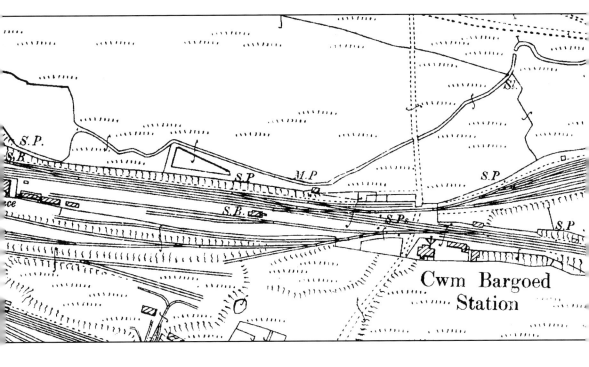

Cwm Bargoed Station

107.   Now over 1200ft above sea level, we have no trees in sight. A small crowd of 1½ joins the train for Dowlais (Cae Harris) on 3rd October 1959. The 0-6-2T is no. 5674 and it is at the summit of the seven mile climb at 1 in 40 to 42. (G.Adams/M.J.Stretton coll.)

108. The signal box had 40 levers and was in use until 21st February 1965. It is seen from a down train on 10th July 1958. There had been up to 20 men here in the early 1920s, but it was 10 in the late 1930s. (H.C.Casserley)

109.   A railtour visited the site on 23rd October 1982, it having been organised by the Monmouthshire Railway Society. Fochriw Colliery was almost one mile distant and around 2300 men were employed there in 1924. (D.H.Mitchell)

110.   No. 37796 arrives with empties from Aberthaw Power Station on 29th June 1993. This can burn material with only 14% volatile content, thus former spoil tips are being consumed. Many date back to the 1820s and arose from the work in numerous pits, adits and mines. Much opencast working is now undertaken. (B.Robbins)

PENYDARREN PLATFORM

111.   Penydarren platform was high on the hillside above Merthyr Tydfil. It was used by workmen between 1928 and 1954. By 1839, Dowlais had 17 iron furnaces, while Penydarren had six. Its famous "tram road" followed. A pair of 37s head for Dowlais with a special about 1982. (P.Jones)

SOUTH OF DOWLAIS

112.   Seen from a train on 17th August 1963, is the 1 in 52 descent to Furnace Tops from Dowlais Junction. The RR had once hauled 0.3m tons of ore annually up from the docks in around 1910, 80 to 100 tons being the maximum for one engine. The signal box had 29 levers and lasted until 21st February 1965. (P.J.Garland/R.S.Carpenter)

113.   Few railtours have reached Furnace Tops, but on 26th March 1977 participants were able to gasp at the extent of the inhospitable and scarred landscape of spoil tips, slag heaps and sludge ponds, left by generations of money makers. There was zig-zag trackwork down the hillside from 1875 until 1983. (R.A.Lumber/D.H.Mitchell)

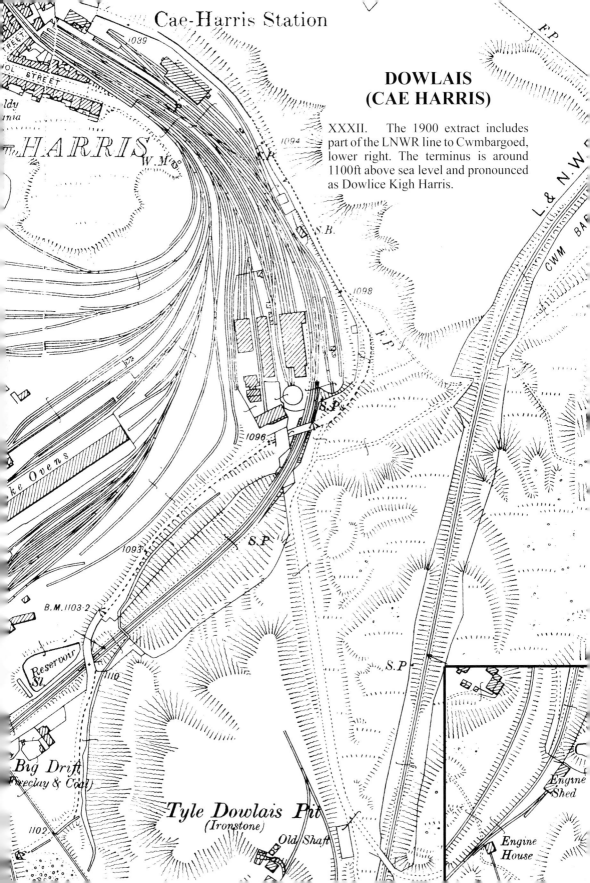

Cae-Harris Station

DOWLAIS
(CAE HARRIS)

XXXII. The 1900 extract includes part of the LNWR line to Cwmbargoed, lower right. The terminus is around 1100ft above sea level and pronounced as Dowlice Kigh Harris.

HARRIS

W. M.

Coke Ovens

S.B.

1098

F.P.

1096

S.B.

L. & N.W.R

CWM BAR

1093

S.P.

B.M. 1103·2

Reservoir

S.P.

1110

Big Drift
(Fireclay & Coal)

Engine Shed

1102

Tyle Dowlais Pit
(Ironstone)

Old Shaft

Engine House

114.   A westward panorama from the Edwardian era is curiously devoid of life, but it does include the massive gates to the station yard. There were 53 employees in 1923, reducing to 23 by 1938; these figures included loco and train crews. (Lens of Sutton coll.)

115.   In this 1922 photograph, we have two platforms and two docks, plus some two-axle stock and a single-axle cart. The track on the left leads to the main industrial complex of steelworks. (D.K.Jones coll.)

116.   Guest Keen & Nettlefold's 0-4-0 no. 2 is about to cross the main road, shown on the left of the map, on 2nd September 1957. The Hudswell Clarke loco was new that year and will soon enter the massive steelworks complex. (M.Dart/Transport Treasury)

117.   The desolate and deformed landscape is evident again as we examine the locomotive depot on 10th July 1958, when it was coded 88D. The running lines pass through the middle of the site. The old and new coaling facilities are nearest to us. (H.C.Casserley)

118.   A closer look two weeks later reveals a well managed and tidy shed. Present are nos 5672, 5660 and 5671, a type well suited to the severe gradients of the route. (G.Adams/M.J.Stretton coll.)

119.   We leave this unusual location with two broad panoramas from August 1963, the year before closure, although goods service would be lost on 7th October of that year. (P.J.Garland/R.S.Carpenter)

120.   The 49-lever signal box (right) closed on 21st February 1965 and the loco shed closed in December 1964. The local environment was in great contrast to the distant Brecon Beacons of great beauty. (P.J.Garland/R.S.Carpenter)

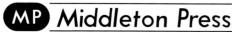
MP Middleton Press

Easebourne Lane, Midhurst, West Sussex.
GU29 9AZ Tel:01730 813169

EVOLVING THE ULTIMATE RAIL ENCYCLOPEDIA
www.middletonpress.co.uk email:info@middletonpress.co.uk
A-978 0 906520 B- 978 1 873793 C-978 1 901706 D-978 1 904474 E- 978 1 906008

OOP Out of print at time of printing - Please check availability BROCHURE AVAILABLE SHOWING NEW TITLES